The Story of the
STATUE OF LIBERTY

Miss Liberty was to be a symbol of friendship of two nations, a gift from the French — children, artists, composers, rich people and poor — to all Americans.

Auguste Bartholdi began by making a 36-foot model, marking it off into 300 parts to be enlarged and made separately. As the model grew in the courtyard of his studio it looked down on the roofs of Paris. Twenty newsmen were entertained for lunch in the knee of the model.

Miss Liberty proper was a lady of parts. Her head went to the Paris World's Fair in a sturdy wagon pulled by twelve horses.

Her finished arm, with an index finger taller than a man, was sent to America for the one-hundredth anniversary of American independence.

Finished at last, she arrived in America in 214 crates.

Now she lifts her lamp "beside the golden door." More than a symbol of friendship, she has come to stand for freedom for the whole world.

The story of the

STATUE OF LIBERTY

By Natalie Miller

Illustrations by Lucy and John Hawkinson

CHILDRENS PRESS, Chicago

Library of Congress Catalog Card Number: 65-12216

Copyright © 1965, Childrens Press

All rights reserved. Printed in the U.S.A.

Published simultaneously in Canada

28 29 R 93 92

Auguste Bartholdi, the young French sculptor, closed his Paris studio early one hot summer day in 1865.

He had been invited to dinner at the home of the famous professor and writer, Edouard de Laboulaye. He did not want to be late. He knew some of the most important men in France would be there, and he felt honored to be invited too.

He put on his best frock coat, brushed his black beard and took the little train that wheezed its way to Versailles, near where Laboulaye lived.

5

All evening he listened quietly to the talking. The talk turned to America. The men were saying that both France and the United States loved freedom and liberty. They remembered how the French had fought side by side with the Americans to help them win their independence.

"If ever a monument is built to celebrate American independence," cried Laboulaye rising from his chair, "it should be built by the work of both countries."

All the men agreed.

A monument grand enough to be the work of two nations! Auguste's heart beat faster. Could he be chosen to make such a monument?

After all, he reasoned, he was known all over France for his statues. He had won the medal of the Legion of Honor for his last huge statue in his native town of Colmar.

He dared not speak out that night, but he planned to speak to Laboulaye at the first good chance.

Before the right moment came, however, France was at war with Prussia. All the time Bartholdi was fighting in the army, he did not forget about the statue.

After the war he visited Laboulaye, and they talked over the whole idea of the statue. Laboulaye suggested that Auguste go to America to see what the people over there thought about it.

Before he left for the United States, he went to Colmar to see his mother. The town had been given to the Germans at the close of the war. He was shocked to find her living on only the third floor of their big old house. German soldiers were living in the rest of the house.

He did not want to leave her, but in her quiet, firm way she told him to go. She showed him that she was quite comfortable and safe, and he could do nothing to help Colmar at that time.

When he saw how the soldiers treated the tall, proud lady in her rustling black gowns — almost as though she were a queen — he agreed to leave.

11

On board ship he drew some sketches for his statue, but none of the ideas pleased him. He threw them overboard and watched the seagulls swoop down on them to see if they were good to eat.

On the morning the ship arrived in New York, Auguste went on deck to catch his first sight of the city. Before him spread a busy inland harbor crowded with ships. Guarding the entrance was tiny Bedloe's Island.

"That is where I want my statue," cried Bartholdi excitedly. "On that island. I shall call it 'Liberty Enlightening the World!'"

Suddenly he knew exactly how she should look. He hurried to his cabin for his sketch pad.

By the time the ship docked he had drawn a calm, proud lady in a long robe with a crown on her head. In her right hand, she held high a torch. In her left, she carried a tablet with July 4, 1776 on it.

For his model, he used the memory of his mother. Who could be a better model, he thought, than the grand lady in Colmar who was honored even by the enemy?

He showed his sketches to many important Americans, even President Grant. They all were eager to have a monument to liberty by the two nations. They felt if France would give the statue, America would gladly give the pedestal on which it would stand.

When he returned to France, Auguste's friend, Laboulaye, planned another dinner. Many of the same men were invited who were there in 1865, when the idea had been born.

Bartholdi told them about his trip to America and showed them a clay model of his statue of liberty.

He explained he wanted it to be the largest statue in the world. The men liked the plans. They formed a committee to raise the money and told him to go ahead with his idea.

Happily, Bartholdi had the studio made larger so that he could build his big lady right there in Paris.

He asked his friend Alexandre Eiffel to make a "skeleton" for her so she would not topple over in a storm.

The French people were happy to raise money for a gift for their sister country. School children gave their small coins and rich men gave large sums. There were carnivals with puppet shows, and fairs with contests.

Famous artists gave paintings to sell. Charles Gounod, the composer, wrote a song about Miss Liberty and presented it at the Paris Opera.

One day a member of the committee went to the studio. He found Bartholdi on a scaffold two stories high, working on a model of the lady that was going to be thirty-six feet tall.

When the sculptor came down, the man said, "The 100th anniversary of American independence is next year. Do you think you can finish Miss Liberty in time for the big celebration fair in Philadelphia?"

Bartholdi shook his head sadly. He pointed to the rough model of the statue that was already taller than most of the houses near it.

"The real Miss Liberty will be four times as large as this one," he said. "We must mark this model off in three hundred parts. Each one will be carefully measured and made larger. After that we must make a plaster cast — then a wooden one. Then we must hammer a hundred tons of copper over that, to be as smooth as skin."

"Enough, enough," cried the committeeman. "I understand why it cannot be finished."

"I will try to have the arm holding the torch ready," said Bartholdi. "That will be taller than this statue here and would show the Americans that we really are getting our gift ready."

The man seemed satisfied and left smiling.

In August of 1876, the arm arrived in Philadelphia. When it was put together, 900,000 people stopped to admire it. Many climbed the steps to the platform around the torch and waved to their friends below.

They marveled to see Miss Liberty's index finger that was taller than a man, and her fingernail an inch wider than a foot ruler.

After the arm was finished and shipped to America, Bartholdi had his workmen begin on the statue's head. Many sightseers came each day. They marveled to see the men looking like dwarfs, running up the scaffolding to pound on a lip a yard wide or shape a single curl higher than a room.

Miss Liberty's head was finished in time to go to the Paris World Fair in 1878.

Bartholdi walked nervously beside the sturdy wagon pulled by twelve strong horses, that carried its precious cargo to the fair grounds.

Mr. Eiffel's men built the framework, or "skeleton," on a big platform in the studio courtyard. Soon Miss Liberty began to rise above the housetops.

One day twenty newsmen were invited to the studio. Bartholdi quickly led them through piles of wire and copper to a door in the lady's sandal. Up, up, up they climbed. Huffing and puffing, the newsmen were glad to stop on a platform, where they found a table set with dishes.

"Gentlemen," said Bartholdi, "I welcome you to lunch in the knee of my big daughter, Liberty."

The food was raised by pulleys from the ground far below. The light came from the blue sky above.

In 1884, the statue was finished. She stood looking down on the roofs of Paris, waiting patiently to go to her new home. But her home was not ready for her.

The people in America did not understand that Miss Liberty was a gift to all the American people. They thought it was a lighthouse for New York City and did not want to pay for the pedestal. It was New York's gift, they said.

The fund committee held festivals, carnivals, and plays. Still there was not enough money.

Work began on the pedestal on Bedloe's Island but was stopped because the money was gone.

Joseph Pulitzer, editor of the *World* newspaper, decided something should be done about it. He wrote articles in his paper asking for donations no matter how small. He persuaded newspaper editors in other towns to do the same. At last, thanks to Mr. Pulitzer, there was enough money to finish the pedestal.

When the good news reached Paris, the huge statue was taken down piece by piece and packed carefully in 214 crates. She was put aboard the *SS Isere,* and in June, 1884, she left for America.

Paris was not long without its own Statue of Liberty. Bartholdi gave the 36-foot model he had used for measuring to some Americans living in Paris. They had it cast in bronze, and it now stands on the Isle de Cygnes in Paris.

When the *Isere* arrived in America, ninety vessels with banners streaming and flags flying escorted her into New York Harbor.

The pedestal which had to be very big and solid to hold the Lady, was not finished. So she was stored on Bedloe's Island while she waited.

When the last stone of the base was swung into place, the workmen showered coins from their pockets into the wet mortar because they were so happy.

Then came the hard task of putting Miss Liberty together. The people on the shore watched curiously as each day the strange skeleton rose higher into the sky. Next came the copper "skin."

The dedication of the statue was set for October 28, 1886. It was a cold, rainy day. But that did not keep away the thousands who lined the streets to watch the long parade.

Bartholdi, standing next to President Cleveland, enjoyed every bit of it. He did not even mind when they found there would not be time for lunch before going to the island for the dedication ceremony.

At 2 o'clock Bartholdi climbed the steps to the top of his "Statue of Liberty Enlightening the World." He waited impatiently for the signal to pull the cord that would drop the Tricolor of France from her face.

When he heard a round of applause far below, during Senator Evart's speech, he thought it was his signal. He pulled the cord.

When the hundreds of gayly decorated ships in the harbor saw Miss Liberty's face, they tooted their whistles and rang their bells all at once. Cannons boomed and bands played. No one heard the end of Mr. Evart's speech.

Since that time Miss Liberty, who began as a sign of the friendship of two nations, has come to mean freedom for the whole world.

People forget she is a statue and look on her as a real person.

Immigrants coming to America to find a new life, look on her as a friend showing them the way to the land of freedom and a better life.

In 1956 the name of the island was changed to Liberty Island. At the bottom of the statue there is a Museum of Immigration.

She is the largest and the best-loved statue in the whole world. She has had her picture taken thousands of times. Many songs and poems have been written about her.

The best-known poem is one called *The New Colossus*, or *Mother of Exiles*. Emma Lazarus wrote it in 1883. The poem closes with the famous words that many school children learn:

Give me your tired, your poor,
Your huddled masses yearning to breathe free,
The wretched refuse of your teeming shore.
Send these, the homeless, tempest-tost, to me,
I lift my lamp beside the golden door!